THAT BEAUTY IN
THE TREES

SOUTHERN MESSENGER POETS

Dave Smith, Series Editor

THAT BEAUTY IN THE TREES

RON SMITH

POEMS

LOUISIANA STATE
UNIVERSITY PRESS
BATON ROUGE

Published by Louisiana State University Press
lsupress.org

LSU Press Paperback Original

DESIGNERS: Michelle A. Neustrom
TYPEFACE: Arno Pro

COVER IMAGE: *Maymont's Japanese Garden X,* 2018, by Emma Knight

LIBRARY OF CONGRESS CATALOGING-IN-PUBLICATION DATA
Names: Smith, Ron, 1949 February 12– author.
Title: That beauty in the trees : poems / Ron Smith.
Description: Baton Rouge : Louisiana State University Press, [2023] |
    Series: Southern messenger poets
Identifiers: LCCN 2022036855 (print) | LCCN 2022036856 (ebook) |
    ISBN 978-0-8071-7798-3 (paperback) | ISBN 978-0-8071-7990-1 (pdf) |
    ISBN 978-0-8071-7987-1 (epub)
Subjects: LCGFT: Poetry.
Classification: LCC PS3569.M537963 B43 2023 (print) | LCC PS3569.
    M537963 (ebook) | DDC 811/.54—dc23/eng/20220804
LC record available at https://lccn.loc.gov/2022036855
LC ebook record available at https://lccn.loc.gov/2022036856

This book is dedicated

with sweeping, indestructible love

to

Delores

People who are always in praise and pursuit of the beautiful are an embarrassment, like people who make a constant display of their religious faith. Somehow, we feel, such things should be kept for our exalted moments, and not paraded in company, or allowed to spill out over dinner.

—ROGER SCRUTON

Poetry might be defined as the clear expression of mixed feelings.

—W. H. AUDEN

CONTENTS

THE ENEMY TO THE SOUTH

EXHIBITION

THAT BEAUTY

ACKNOWLEDGMENTS

I am grateful to the editors of the following periodicals and anthologies, in which these poems first appeared. Some poems have been revised since their first appearance, and some titles have changed.

American Journal of Poetry: "Public Servant, Country Squire"; *Artemis:* "The Assisi Poem, Finally," "EP in the Garden," "Hilda Was Too Tall for a Washable Frock," "Lucky Strike," and "Riefenstahl," "Troilos"; *Art Meets Literature:* "Bouguereau's Big Bow-Wow"; *Art & Poetry Gallery Guide:* "Franz Kline's *Zinc Yellow* (1959)"; *Arts of War & Peace* (Université Paris Diderot): "*Estadio Guillermón Moncada*," "I Always Thought I'd Die, "Lily, Her Men," and "Mezzogiorno" (in English and Italian); *Blackbird:* "Orvieto"; *Broad Street:* "Drought, Rome," "Short Straw," "Suitor," and "Volterra"; *A Compendium of Kisses:* "Looking into Milano"; *Ezra's Book:* "Berth of Modern Poetry," "Curse Tablet," and "Master"; *English Journal:* "Last Autumn"; *Five Points:* "'He Loved the World He Fought to Save'"; *Into Quarterly:* "The South"; *Lingering in the Margins: A River City Poets Anthology:* "Local Color"; *Make It New:* "Salamanca"; *Now and Then:* "Away"; *A Packet of Poems for Ezra Pound:* "Exhibition"; *Plume Poetry* (anthologies): "Catullus," "Eric Blair's Wall," "How She Came to Be a Model," "[Paris] [New York] [Philadelphia]," and "Poe in Rome"; *Plume* (online): "Don't Know Much About the French I Took," "Home Front," "Remedios Varo's *Locomotión Capilar* (1959)," "Rizal Stadium, World War II," "Rome/Glasgow: Early March," and "This Moment"; *POETiCA REViEW:* "The Ancrene Wisse"; *Poetry Northwest:* "That Beauty in the Trees"; *Sport Literate:* "All-Boys School . . ."; *Style Weekly:* "How It Was" and "Over."

Thanks also to the editors of periodicals, anthologies, and online sites where some of the above poems have been reprinted.

Aethlon: "Away"; *Artemis:* "Home Front," "Volterra," "Over," and "This Moment"; *Broad Street:* "Don't Know Much About the French I Took" and "Suitor"; *Make It New:* "Berth of Modern Poetry" [in English & Italian], "EP in the Garden," and "Hilda Was Too Tall for a Washable Frock"; *Mount Vernon Magazine:* "Suitor"; *Poetry Daily:* "Volterra"; *Poets Speaking to Poets: Echoes & Tributes:* "E.P. in the Garden"; *Style Weekly:* "Local Color" and "That Beauty in the Trees."

Thanks is especially due to Amherst Glebe Arts Response for commissioning "Orvieto" for musical settings; to the Chrysler Museum of Art, for its inspiring Poetry & Art Day; to the Virginia Museum of Fine Arts for commissioning the poem "Troilos" (and others) for a reading at the exhibition "The Horse in Ancient Greek Art"; to Susann Cokal at *Broad Street* for nominating "Volterra" for a Pushcart Prize; to the Library of Virginia & Virginia Museum of Fine Arts for commissioning "Bouguereau's Big Bow-Wow"; to the staff at Rome's Keats-Shelley House and at the official residence of the American ambassador for hosting readings and encouraging new work; and to St. Christopher's School for its support of the arts.

THE ENEMY TO THE SOUTH

They make a wilderness and call it peace.

—TACITUS

The world itself can be our desert.

—SAINT AUGUSTINE OF HIPPO

This Moment

You know when darkness seems to pour
from the sky, driving tense
even a mile from your own front door, two black
lanes with a centerline oh
so easy to cross—flashing lights, red in those days:
police. I think I was behind
the wheel but it could have been Royce who
pulled off Augusta Road
between the paved Ten Pin parking lot

and the mud track leading
to the Saratoga Club. We eased onto the mud side
where we'd never been before,
because that's where the crowd was, where something
had happened, cop grinning,
and more than fifty years later I can't say
whether I knew him, though we
had only four then, I think, in Garden City.
All the eyes had that look
eyes have when the ordinary hour breaks open

and shines a spotlight
of extravagance into dark routine. Headlights.
Until this moment—*this moment*—
I have not asked if my own eyes looked like that.
How can it be this moment?
penny loafers, wingtips, Converses arced
round a man face down
on the sludgy shoulder. Do I remember
a disappearing rivulet

of blood? I can't ask Royce. He's dead. I seem
to recall a joke about catching
a fender instead of a bus. Saturday night, right
in front of the Saratoga Club.
In my head how can there be only white faces, faces lit
with a kind of joy, jazzy
amusement—an accident, therefore, a gift. And so,
killing time, waiting for the useless
ambulance. To the south, Royce and Bobby and I
clustered often in the parking lot,

palming a beer, sometimes going in to knock down
a few pins, but mostly circling
the nine ball table, talking trash. To the north,
the mythical, mystical
Saratoga Club, set back from the road in year-round
Christmas lights, shadowed
on the weekends with fedoras and long skirts, dark
people keeping their distance
even now, not one kneeling by this utterly still man,
dripping darkness
from black umbrellas, muted music behind them, inside.

I Always Thought I'd Die

in a nuclear wink, would not have time
to know what hit me. Or, after
distant flashes and the shock waves, slowly
of radiation sickness, combs full of hair,
bleeding from the eyes, fingernails,
nostrils, anus. After the president's head detonated,
I walked the mile home

                         from history class,
dusty concrete along Augusta Road, scanning
the sky for the first needle-glints of Russian missiles.
But it was just Oswald, a mere ten years older
than I was, I know now, son of one Robert E. Lee,
a marine, like my father—like Lee O. himself—but dead
before the boy was born.

                         Young Oswald thought
god was a dog, a star, rats. His smiling chinstrapped
mug looks a lot like my teammates'
Wells and Strobo, who both joined the Corps right
after high school, got themselves killed
in short order. Oswald was in radar, a word
he couldn't get wrong.

                         Like my father
he qualified sharpshooter. Like my father
he was honorably discharged. Unlike my father
he didn't deserve it. He never killed anybody
until he did Kennedy and Tippet. He never
boxed, he never looked like Clark Gable.
My father believed

                            somebody on the grassy knoll
did it, even though he knew about the trip
to Moscow. He slashed his left wrist. He met
a girl with a Shakespearean handle, fathered
a kid he named after a summer month,
came home a family man, purchased
an Italian rifle

                            created within a few miles
of the Shroud of Turin. Unlike my father,
who sweated in thick Savannah air hugging
creosote poles, Lee found it hard
to hold a job. I have looked out that window.
Despite what you have heard, it was
an easy shot.

                        My father killed several men
on what he always called The Island. It wasn't easy
with an M1903, certainly not with a bayonet, never
had second thoughts about Hiroshima. They boarded
a stinking troop train for San Diego, waited
all day in the Carolina heat, were ordered
back to barracks.

                         No A-bomb, no Ronnie Smith,
he said, a million marines, soldiers, sailors, fly boys—
a million would have bought the farm
on the mainland. He figured his number was up,
but, boom, boom, the war was over. He took
his malaria to Chatham County, married an operator
with the middle name Lee,

                              and sired, as they say,
me. And though my Uncle Don, skinny and jumpy
as Lee Harvey himself, rolled hundreds of warheads

from Travis Field to Hunter Air Force Base
about the time I turned twelve—by convoy right
through the heart of my hometown, down
what is now MLK Boulevard—

                          looks like I'll make
three score years and ten. Haven't been vaporized
or particularly irradiated, far as I know. 1Y'ed out
of Vietnam, despite football. It wasn't the concussions
or the trick shoulders, knees, arthritic feet, hips, spine.
Blood pressure off the chart, the doc growled.
No Hiroshimas in my lifetime. Not yet.

Troilos

Nothing but a boy, soon to be snatched
by the hair from his horse by swift-footed,
cold-hearted Achilles,
a boy compounded
of the founders of Troy, born to be
destroyed by honor-bound Greeks,
men of many reasons.

Why do the Bards not agree? Why must we
rely on potters who show
but don't explain, who leave us to complain
that Achilles, our lion,
was a beast to kill and desecrate
Hecuba's much-loved ephebe?

Here he is, with his sister
Polyxena, who's already dropped and broken
her hydria at Apollo's Thrymba. And *that* god
will have his revenge, will
move the pretty boy Paris—
like every coward safely

out of range—to bring down Peleus's son
with a flimsy arrow.
Therefore, beheaded, mutilated, Troilos's beautiful body
must anger the gods, Achilles be handed over
to his ambiguous fame.
Over Troilos, Trojans will wail.

And the gods?
                    They will shake their magnificent,
          immortal heads, forget their outrage,
                              and go their ways,
                heedless of the sorrows
of fighters and farmers, of men and women,
                    of boys and girls who strive and grieve
                and, as is their habit, in their weakness, simply die.

Franz Kline's *Zinc Yellow* (1959)

Ah! My high school's
colors, gold and black,
colors of conflict and conquest,
loot and loss,
extremes not too far
from black and white.
"Everthang's not black and white,"
teachers, parents loved
to say, but they didn't mean it. And now I see
the black is low, pushing in
from the left, slashing
at the bright monolith
towering above it, brightness
leaning over it as if to say,
"Hold it right there, Blackness,"
or maybe hunching
forward from the blow
to its midsection where
now I see the monolith
begins to break up, shows
a wound of darkness at its golden heart,
smidge of black on its
back heel, lower right—
the corner opposite
that little wash of light
blue-cloudless sky,
I'll choose to think, or sky dissolved
in the marsh water of Savannah, in
the fifties or sixties when I was golden
and noble Joby Wright was nothing

but a black boy
who must have hated my guts
in the bad old days
in my, in his
hometown.

Curse Tablet

May the bony man
who snatched my carry-on
from the rental car
suffer major dental scars
as well as self-administered
feculent catheters for an STD
contracted after reading
the handwritten poems therein
aloud to a bleeding
whore he finds next to a garbage bin
on the Via Appia Antica
near the aeroporto. May
he mangle even the sonnet
with a tongue with an abscess on it.

Catullus

"Turds!" he said. "The wine is watered! For all
 your gall, you refined Roman weenies
can't drink with a real Gaul."
                    Emptied the bowl anyway,
 smelling sulphur, knowing it was only
  in his mind, singed air of Vulcan
   in rainy Verona
where his brother lay dead not far from the new forum
                    paved with mud.

  In the consulship of Julius and
                    Caesar this foul maze of a city
never enough radishes, for mouths
   or anuses. *Oh, Lesbia! How
 did I ever get tangled with you, my hate,
      my love?* In his dreams: large towns
  dilapidated and depilated, plucked and scattered
   by transalpine Gauls,
the *real* thing, sloshed with beer and god-knows
                    what else, their fists full of radishes . . .

  He has to clear his head.
      Bithynia's soft ground
   swallowed Rome's new temples. How hot
their flesh together, slicked with sweat and oils,
      but she was never quite there
   no matter what part of him
was in her mouth, her other mouths . . .
                    Dregs in the cloudy wine . . .

. . . never quite daylight
in her eyes. Teeth marks
on his shoulder, showers
of nuts as the bride squealed like sail ropes
on the Black Sea.
"Walnuts and turds," he said
in a rockslide of cisalpine syllables.
"Pour me another.
And hold your water."

Rome/Glasgow: Early March

Our favorite time to visit—cool air for all-day walking, in
the twisting vicoli or mile after mile along Via Appia Antica,
parrots in the pines—majestic umbrella pines—puntarelle with
anchovy sauce, fried artichokes, gusts of garlic on every street,
the nearly painful excitement of escaping winter, sidewalk
saxophones, the jazz and noise and energy and tangles of
tongues and vibrant confusion of it all—this time, we found our
(yes, *our*) eternally crowded Eternal City bloated with beefy men
in kilts, roaring red-faced over mugs of beer with their substantial
companions in the ristoranti in Campo de' Fiori, the tables in front of
the Pantheon, above, below, all over the Spanish Steps, blocking
the entrance to Keats's final flat, from Trastevere and Testaccio
to Prati and Parioli, happy, boisterous, large-calved stereotypes
from a hundred movies, wannabe Bravehearts, all. Clouds
of costumed clichés floating like Macy's Day Parade balloons
through the cobbled streets . . .
                              Finally, in the Piazza Navona,
I strolled up to a guy planting a beefy butt on the edge
of the Neptune Fountain. I was thinking of breaking the ice
by telling the pink behemoth they used to call it Fontana dei
Calderari, because it was so close to the blacksmith shops,
pots and pans pounded by brawny men of yesteryear in heat
like that I saw beginning to bloom in his considerable cheeks.
I tried to sound casual and friendly: "Where you from?"
Over the foaming mug in his fist he took me in. "Where
do ya think I'm from?" "Well," I said, suave as David Niven,
"I live in Virginia, you can see a lot of kilts in Richmond." He
looked me up and down. "Glasgow," he growled. Not missing
a beat, I praised Rennie MacKintosh and the lovely country walks
all round his populous city, babbling about White Cart "Water"
and the Rotten Calder River and hollow dingles and such. I
mentioned Saint Mungo. I even used the word linn for waterfall

and the word gushet for a road junction—which allowed me to
segue to the glorious howling traffic madness that was Rome. I
used a word our landlady on the Isle of Skye taught me:
hoaching.

   The whole time this jumbo joke in a kilt and sporran
and a tam-o-can-you-believe it-shanter stared at me as if *I*—in my
blue blazer and button-down shirt—were some kind of skeevy varmint.
"Why so many Glaswegians in Rome? You guys are everywhere."
A swollen infestation, I might have said. "Football," he said—then,
as if speaking to a half-witted child: "Rugby." Really? Consequently,
flashed upon my inner eye another stereotype: A supercilious
gigolo dangling an insouciant cigarette, mesmerizing
a soccer ball with an expensive pointed shoe, his haughty,
head-tossing inamorata coolly appraising him—the *last* guy
you're likely to see in the messy mayhem of a manly scrum.
"Italy has a *rugby* team?" "Oh, yeah, and they're very good,"
he said with a frown. "You gallus boys won't have any trouble,"
I said, like a goddamn fool. "You can handle these wine-sippers
like a wheely bin."

   His mouth fell open, but he had the presence
of mind to lift his mug to me. I envisioned a contest in Foro Italico's
Stadio dei Marmi, a bloody maelstrom of Malkies that spattered
gore and fine Italian brains all over Mussolini's effete marble
musclemen. Of course they'd be playing farther upstream
in the Stadio Flaminio, not far from the Milvian Bridge,
where Constantine conjured that dead wizard Jesus to rout
Maxentius and steal the empire's throne. The Tiber was choked
with valiant bodies. But those were *real* Romans.

   I didn't think
about the match *once* that night as we lounged in Giggetto's
with a crock of transcendent eggplant parmigiana,
linguine con vongole, and a liter of house white—after, of course,
our puntarelle and procuitto e formaggio. Espresso and Limoncello
and then weaving home, not a kilt or tartan plaid in sight, just
slim locals and a few drunk Germans.

　　　　　　　　　　　　　Next night, the cafés
and trattorias and osterias were congested with muted, morose
Scotsmen and their somewhat less muted wives. Some licked
or spooned gelato without much pleasure or swallowed
absent-mindedly supplì or porchetta. One couple sat brooding
over cacio e pepe and carbonara that was getting cold. A few
of the old ones were simply stupefied, eyes wide. I remember
in particular in Piazza della Rotonda four corpulent Celts
gulping whiskey, gazing round with a wild surmise, silent,
flabbergasted, high and not at all dry upon what might
just as well have been a peak in Darien.

Estadio Guillermón Moncada

Santiago de Cuba

The brisk, beautiful women in military green
would rather be somewhere else. Right now, this
   is the only place I'll ever want to be.
Box seat, left field line, a day blazing and humid,
   marble galleons sailing the blue,
       serene stone armada floating
   above the stadium, camphor and tobacco,
rum and sweat sweetening the breeze.

       The hometown boys are the Bees,
   Avispas, Santiago hosting Havana, Mets
   who visit this time-warp
honoring a local hero who took his mother's name
       because the father he loved
   had been a slave.
Writer, carpenter, Brigadier General,
   black as electrical tape on a baseball bat,
he attacked the sugar mill in La Guerra Chiquita

and became a Major General.
       I jumbled it all down in a tiny pad
in a jolting ride from a bar
       hazy with historians and fabulists.
   The bewitching militia
has its eyes on us, two Americans, three Slovaks,
       and an old Cuban
   who looks more like a farmer

than a sports fan. He's following the play-by-play
   on a battered Motorola in his lap.
   Or is he, with that earpiece,

a government spy?
Josh grumbles again he'd rather see a bullfight.
             Those alluring, impassive eyes . . . What
are they watching for? You can feel them
                         pass over you like a searchlight.
             Bright red halfsmiles, the Bees

behind them warming up in red and smudged white,
             the Mets solid red—gleaming combat boots
                         they could use to check their eyeliner,
unlike the players' dusty cleats, old, even cracked.
             There's only one first-base glove
             for both teams, handed off when the innings change.
             I see no sidearms. Each crisp uniform
                         has a gunmetal patch

             over a swellingly patriotic
                         heart: *Ministerio de Interior.*
             And we are dreaming
of interiors, two Americans, three Slovaks, and a Cuban
             who's not too old to dream, you can
tell by the star in his milky sapphire eye.
             The Bees pitcher
             is having a day. Sliders, changeups thump
into the catcher's mitt, then the leather screams

             at a fastball I didn't even see.
This one's dark eyes drift over us, cools my damp shirt
             with its pocket full of cigars. She rises
and moves toward me, extends her palm for the foul ball
             I one-handed like a kid. I pass
             the scuffed cowhide to her meekly,
                         without a word, awareness and patience
             in those dark eyes, like the eyes

of her countryman who rapped
his knuckles on my passport,
pretending to stamp it. She
looks at me a long moment.
The tall boy waiting at the wall
is the third basemen. I
realize I am holding my breath. She
blinks as if nodding,
then whirls and pops his glove with a laser throw.

The Ancrene Wisse

The introduction of a person's hand
                 into your cell is a penetration.
      You may not cross your legs, affect
         a lisp, arch your eyebrows
with moistened fingers. You may own
      no glove. You must seek permission
             to wear a belt made of hair or iron
or hedgehog skins. You may not flog yourself
         with these things, nor may you
bloody yourself, nor sting yourself with nettles.
         Do not strike the front of your body,
             nor lacerate your flesh in any way.
      All tortures are treats to be rationed,
      permissible only with authorization.

Mezzogiorno

HE SAID:
The head is the North,
the heart is the South.
In between we find the mouth.

I SAID:
The Deep South?

HE SAID:
Mezzogiorno?
The dirty bits,
where you make your babies,
take your shits.
[*smiles*]

I SAID:
And the mouth has teeth
as well as a tongue.

HE SAID:
Which is worse? The bites
or the saying wrong?

I SAID:
Your whole body lies.

HE SAID:
At end of each day, yes,
dies.

First Wave

"HE LOVED THE WORLD HE FOUGHT TO SAVE"

When I suggested it for his tombstone,
the woman selling us Mother's plot said,
"Perfect." A Marine herself, she was firm
when my father said, "But idn't it bad
to put *fought?*"—firm as I was. "Oh, no,"
we said together to the man whose hands
boxing had broken and knotted, a boy who,
at eighteen was one of the first to land
on Guadalcanal. "Must have been hell,"
I said after reading about Omaha Beach.
"Naw," he said. "Getting over the side
of the Higgins Boat was hardest—all that gear.
Beautiful day. Japs just let us wade ashore.
Waiting. Watching. Next morning: Welcome to the war."

SHORT STRAW

Why was that the thing that haunted him
seventy years? Guard duty, whispering,
drawing straws. His strapping friend putting
aside the Springfield, charging the shadow,
thrashing in the dark, grunts, then the groan,
—sickening snap—and my father, eighteen,
tried to pull his friend off the tiny man. "He's
gone, Sammy," he hissed, "he's done, let him go!"
But his brawny friend kept twisting the head,
moaning softly. Given the men he'd personally
dropped, the colonel with his guts in his lap,
gold teeth pried from the gaping, stinking dead,
why was *that* the thing that choked him up,
that made him flinch away from you and me?

Rizal Stadium, World War II

During fighting for Rizal Stadium, [Rod] Serling shot and
killed a Japanese soldier on third base . . .

—FROM THE NATIONAL WORLD WAR II MUSEUM,
NEW ORLEANS

He was almost home, poor guy. Or was he
on his way to the dugout, which almost certainly
they did not have, so on his way
to the locker room door, when a kid same age
as my father zapped him. I want to see him
crouching to steal the plate, or rounding
the bag. Why don't I want to see him
scooping up a grounder when he's
surprised by a bolt-action Springfield?

This poem is not about *The Twilight Zone.*
In six years of baseball I scored so
rarely that stomping that square
into a puff of dust, dust already behind me,
is a dream I have had a thousand times. Brian
Hunter ruined my best chance to steal
the big one. But that's another story. How many

hours did I spend out there sweeping them up,
taking bad hops in the heart then firing a
frozen (yes) frozen rope to first? That could have been
me, if I had been born way back and in Japan.
Yellow Peril—it has a ring to it. But Rod and I
have the same initials—more likely I would
have been the killer, a dark-haired Yank. Get off
my base! What do you know about this game, you
un-American bastard? If I don't kill you, you

might kill my father who's right now fighting
for his life on Guadalcanal. I love horror
and time travel. Besides, you tiny terrors
want to take our jungles from us, our
battleships and manifest destiny. Take
that, you sneak attackers. Even if you were *born*
on third, you would never make it home.

I don't mean to be flippant. This is a sports poem.
It has no place for "the tension, the violence, the
anguish of protracted war," as Serling described it.
The grief. The guilt. My father, an excellent catcher
and hitter with a happy temperament, caught
typhoid and typhus and malaria, but never
had what they quaintly called "battle fatigue."
So he said. Serling did, had screaming nightmares
all his life, but this is a sports poem. Dad
fought heavyweight, Serling flyweight until
a buddy rattled his brains on one or another
Pacific island. Hiking is a sport, but not in all that
gear and combat boots. My father hated walking
to the end of his days. If this were not a sports piece,
I would have room for a found poem. For example,
Serling, introducing Episode 19, speaks of

> the faces of the young men who fight,
> as if some omniscient painter
> had mixed a tube of oils that were
> at one time earth brown, dust gray,
> blood red, beard black, and fear—yellow white . . .

On Leyte—and you'll see how this fits—Serling starved
pulling demolition duty, when, thank God, crates
of food fell like manna from the sky, most under
parachutes. His pal Melvin Levy exulted, arms out

like Jesus, till one crate took off his head. Literally.
This might remind you of Machiavelli's and Pope Leo X's
spectator delight at peasants gleefully catching barrels
full of living pigs rolled down Monte Testaccio, as I say
in a poem, "like the drunks at Daytona trying to catch
the cars as they roar around the track." Crate-catching,
we could call Melvin Levy's sport. Except that it wasn't
a sport at all or even solemn combat. It was one of those
accidents that happen when young men gather
to do whatever it is they do in their youthful energy
and innocence. Like a hamstring pulled tagging up
after that long, long fly is somehow snagged in center,
but you, at least, manage to limp home.

Lily, Her Men

She laughed down at me
    wobbling at the curb in the suffocating heat
of tourist D.C., the White House wavering
      in the white mist of her hair.
She was planted solid as the Holy Church of God.
    Later, linebacker, I believed
I had become a man. She drove me to my knees
        in front of her daughter's stove, bending
    my fingers back to my wrists. "You think
you stronger than me?"
      She made me beg. My face burned for a week.
      Much as she loved me,
she knew about men.

    Seven children sit
    on the side of the ditch.
    That whining sound
    is the saw she works to cut up the logs.
    And that brutal clucking is the ax.
    She feeds her babies
    the heat of a Georgia summer.
    They drink her sour sweat for decades.
    Then John Kennedy puts her up
    near the sky. She gives him the power
    because he's so good looking.
    Her two rooms shine with the cloud-light
    of her humility and her fear of dirt shame.
    She puts a wedge of lemon pie in front of me.
    She takes the coffee cup right out of my hand
    and washes it. She saw Jesus last week,
    but he didn't see her. Some days
    the elevator doesn't work.

The boys get up out of that ditch and walk down that dirt road
                    until they smudge and shrivel into tramps. Oscar,
oldest, dies first. Carl paints houses when he's sober enough
                to get most of the paint on the walls.
                                    Few can see past the smiles
before the panes are painted over. Then, he loads up
                    the empty bottles, leaves the cans full of color, pockets
            whatever they sever him with, and drives
                    weaving away, speckled all over like Atlanta in autumn.
    Haskell gets half eaten by the paper mill
and takes the other half out behind the projects
                    and drinks it up. He'll leave that trailer
        once, for Aunt Ag's funeral. His daughter will carry him home
            and hose him down.

Howard lugs lead type
        at the *Morning News* till computers turn all the words into thoughts
                        and the boys dump him in a vat of Old Hickory.
    He sleeps under the clothesline. He's been there
                long enough to get sunburned, but since it's Savannah,
                    thunder will rumble at four o'clock, lightning
        will tear each black cloud wide open so the rain can come down hard,
            like a skillet. When it hits him
                he will come up explaining he didn't know
            what time it was.

And this is their father's thin, lined face: Clisby's thirty-five and almost
sober. Now he's fifty, comes home one bright afternoon covered with
oily filth from sleeping under a tractor trailer parked near Pinkey's.
He's awake long enough to suffer home under the Spanish moss. Yes,
he *is* going to curl up on that white bedspread Lily's sold a year of
breakfasts to buy. She hits him across the shoulders with the electric
iron, she hits him on an elbow as he scrambles toward the window
quoting Howard, more or less, on the surprises visited upon the
innocence of sleep. That twanging lilt's his own special love of the profane

and obscene. She hits him till he jumps from the second-floor balcony,
breaks his ankle on the sidewalk. She'll hit him again when he comes
through that door from the hospital, and then she'll stay up all night
putting wet cloths on this or that part of him. What a woman, he'll say.
She'll feed him half a chicken.

Lily lives now in half a room
        in Mayor Fountain's Home
under the viaduct. The mayor also owns the mortuary
           right next door and his first name is Cleave.
She knows he's the devil.
              Today, she holds hands with Brother Butler
who's holding hands with Jesus who has long hair
        and a beard, but he's Jesus and you're not.
     You just look dirty. Brother Butler hangs
on the only nail they'll let her put in the bright lime sheetrock walls.

    Lily's forgotten her sons' names because
    the walls are lemon now. Brother Butler fell
    and the devil put that crack across his face.
    Those cards where the sun ought to be
    came from her grandchildren and she'll remember
    their dance recitals and football teams
    if you give her enough time.

You give her enough time. She swings the ax.
      She places a wedge of sunlight on her eldest's tongue,
    his eyes bright as sapphires. You'd never know
he's going to hell. The girls line up one by one
      in their only dresses, yellow and white. They will never smile
in a row again. She swings the ax.

    A naked man rises from the bloody wound
    in the pine log. He smells like vomit. *You* take
    a goddamn shower. Now he's Clisby, only he's

not drunk and he's gentle, thinking about where
he wants to put his fingers, putting them there
as if he cares whether she cares. She won't do
that. She won't do that, either, but it's Clisby
filling her up with the future. Inside the bright
cloud, she takes off her strong fingers one by one,
like removing a glove. She knows that ditch.
It fed her children. She can get used to it,
the beard. Kiss me again, Jesus. Make me like it.

Eric Blair's Wall

Our Tory Anarchist boiled in the bully against the brick—the Wall Game scrum the bully. Not for him the playing fields of Eton, only this warped offspring of rugby, bricks abrading cheeks, elbows, knees, aristocratic rabble on its way to Oxford, Cambridge, except for Blair, self snatched from a Sussex river he liked to fish (another sport with few rules), shielding his proper parents from his Boolean *OR*-ness, armpit truths, astringent facts, hard head always smack up against unyielding identicals—alternative to grow into. The road to Wigan Pier went through Burma, where he was the Wall, Burmese criminals the scrum, the scum, the bully, the occasionally hanged. Shot an elephant, harmless wall of a creature, because a mob craved a glimpse of empire in its teenage cop. A good hater, now he hated himself, wore what I call a Hitler mustache. At the Aragon Front, it was "unspeakably cold" when he got over a pissant wall for a few seconds, was, shortly thereafter thank God, shot by a fascist sniper before a communist could drill him in the back. Eton's Wall's furrow: 15 by 110 meters, along a barrier articulated in the Enlightenment. A wall's a team, but a bully's the chaos inside a boy, whose aim's to keep you from forming the tunnel that could funnel the ball toward your calx. Periscope of a man, bullet zipping through delicate mesh of neck—out of action at just the right time, reluctant imperialist, skeptical communist, Edwardian revolutionary—weak lungs of Eric Blair, fired brick of George Orwell, wall and boy, immovable object, flimsy flesh, firm *no* to Auden's "necessary murder"—men lying everywhere, lying men shooting everybody, everybody shooting everybody else, in Barcelona. I have seen the Ministry of Truth; his wife worked there, not far from his desk at the BBC, by now his mustache thin as a knife blade and so was he. Flagpole, he looked down his nose at you and me, director or drudge, only literally, saw the Age of Reason curved into enclosure, was the tramp and the policeman who moved the tramp along. I don't know what it walled in or out. He was on the ownership side, King's Scholar, whose realm Oppidans invaded twice a year, pouring over the wall. Spectators saw a bunch of butts, rarely a ball. Goals? One a decade. You may push your fist into a player's face but not furk or sneak. I, too, have been a guardian of tradition and meaningless mayhem. In the only film of Blair, we see him marching arm-in-arm with his team, every boy in a long scarf and a cap. They are a wall approaching a wall. I can't be sure, but every one seems to be smiling. And there's our man, fourth from the left, towering above his peers, head high, and I swear smiling.

Founder

SUITOR

She liked him, though she knew exactly
what he was after, this tower of a man, topped
        with flame. He came galloping up and flowed
from the saddle with a dignified grace,
        flushed, perhaps from the sun, and
looked her straight in the eye. She wanted
        to put her tiny hand in his prodigious one, but
he bowed, as he always did, and began to speak
oh so carefully, yes, as he always did. Yes, she
        would walk with him. Yes, it *was*
a fine day.

When, to impress her, he had thrown those flat stones
        across the Rappahannock, she thought of Ulysses
among the Phaeacians, the discus
        he threw like the demigod he was. Or was he?
Ulysses, she meant, not this grandly self-conscious
        militia colonel who had returned
from Barbados scarred by the pox. And all
        for nothing. A perfect match,

        her land and his. He always won
at pulling the stick or throwing the bar and
        he could ride, oh he could ride
        like a centaur. Hercules, *he* was
the demigod, not Ulysses who, nevertheless, made
        the Phaeacians flinch when he
        flung the humming disc

out of sight and offered to box or wrestle any of them.
Yes, of course, she would
write to him, for she loved
receiving his courtesies in that
controlled, precise hand. Come again, she said, and
returning his bow (a little ironically), felt
her palms aching, though
she didn't know why.

MASTER

Sir: With this Letter comes a Negro (Tom)
which I beg the favour of you to sell,
in any of the Islands you may go to,
for whatever he will fetch,
& bring me in return for him
One Hdh of best Molasses
One Ditto of best Rum
One barrl of Lymes—if good and Cheap
One Pot of Tamarinds—contg about 10 lbs.
Two small Do of mixed Sweetmeats—abt. 5 lbs. each.
And the residue, much or little,
in good old Spirits. That this fellow

is both a Rogue & Runaway
(tho. he was by no means remarkable for the former,
and never practiced the latter till of late)
I shall not pretend to deny—But he is
exceedingly healthy,
strong, and good at the Hoe, the whole
neighborhood can testifie . . .
which gives me reason to hope he may,
with your good management,
sell well, if kept clean & trim'd up
a little when offerd to Sale.

I shall very chearfully
allow you the customary Commissions on this affair,
and must beg the favour of you
(lest he shoud attempt his escape)
to keep him handcuffd
till you get to Sea—or in the Bay—
after which I doubt not but you may
make him very useful to you. I wish you a pleasant
and prosperous Passage,
and a safe & speedy return,
being Sir, Yr Very Hblc Sert
Go: Washington

PUBLIC SERVANT, COUNTRY SQUIRE

Wiencek never mentions slave teeth
in *An Imperfect God,* a book I recommend if
you think all slavers were the same and Washington
as cruel as the rest. GW, like Shakespeare
always frugal, got even teeth for well
under market price. A proud, ambitious, insecure, simple
man, he told granddaughter Nelly
his time as president was little more

than vanity and vexation. (He felt obliged
to sign our first fugitive slave law.)
That Polish nobleman who imposed
on him for twelve long days said the old man
breakfasted on tea and cakes made
from maize. Because of his teeth,
the noble vagabond said, he spread slices
with butter and honey.

*[Paid 6 Pounds 2 Shillings to Negros for 9 Teeth (George
Washington's Ledger B, 8 May 1784, Library of Congress)]*

Scholar Kathryn Gehred writes (shaped a bit
here—but not, I hope, *distorted*):
As [our] first president,
Washington set the standard for leadership
and the goals of [our] brand-new country. He
made difficult decisions, including to *step down*
from office after two terms, setting
a precedent (thank God),
preventing [our] new democracy from sliding back
into monarchy. At the end of his life,

he also made
the controversial [*sic*] decision (not condoned by
his family) to free *his* portion
of Mount Vernon's slaves. We
can't deny, however—we *can't*—that he also
followed the "standards" of his time,
condon[ing], even encourag[ing]
violence as a way to keep the enslaved sub*servient.*
The great man bought and sold slaves
for *economic* reasons, sometimes, sometimes breaking

("Never trust a scholar who uses the word ' _____.'")

up families. While president, leading
[my] *nominally* free country,
he actively *prevented* his enslaved "servants"
from learning of their own "natural" right to free-
dom. *Ergo:* Without more doc-
umentation that might help us find the *real* story
behind our Founder's dentures,
our reactions to the revelation
that they included human teeth have more to do with our own

worldviews, even subconscious
                    beliefs about our first president,
        than with "historic reality." *All*
                    history involves interpretation and person-
-al bias *but* with a *subject* as
                    fraught [from Middle Dutch *vrachten*,
        from *vracht* 'ship's cargo'] as slavery *and* involving an *icon*
            ("a painting of Jesus Christ or another holy figure")
                like George Washington,
responses can be—*can* be—all the more intense and emotional.

                Stories like *this* provide *us*
        with the op-
                        port-
                unity
        to investigate the evidence, to no-
            tice our re-
                    sponses to that evi-
dence, and finally,
                    perhaps most valuably, to ex-
        amine *why* we are re-
                        spond-
                    ing as we do.

Over

All these years now, and it's over, isn't it,
the hardly sleeping, the dreams
that aren't dreams, and the waking
weight of it? Yes, it's over, long over.

Aren't you glad you didn't see them
in the flesh, the jumpers? Aren't you glad
you didn't take those calls, the we're
dying up here calls? The I just have

time to say I love you calls? When
you saw on your TV the first tower fall,
you said, Of course: How could I not
see that it would fall? But you couldn't,

could you, see that it would fall?
And then you knew the other.
How many months was it that you fell
a thousand feet deafened by the sunlight

on the rooftops, on the river, by the
free howl of flying, or breathless in the
glittering, powdering tons of steel and glass,
of struts and desks and door frames,

dry wall, printers, fax machines, laptops,
coffee cups, fell in a gray storm of shredding,
shredding as you fell, separating, a cloud roar
of black fire and a swarm of edges. Why

didn't you take your daughter to school or
have another bagel somewhere along the way,
show up an hour late like the lucky ones?
Such a beautiful day. Clear enough

all down the East Coast for even
a poor pilot, orienting by the Pentagon's
black plume, to come in low over
the Lincoln Memorial, just miss

the Washington Monument, and vaporize
the Capitol dome. You whispered, It can't
get worse than this. You knew, you know
it can always get worse than this.

How It Was

Since we are surrounded by so great a cloud of witnesses,
let us lay aside every weight and the sin that so easily
ensnares us and let us run with endurance the race
that is set before us.

—HEBREWS 12:1

I.

First, this caped peacock, ridiculous
romantic beard, feather in the fancy hat,
rearing on his horse, turning
in the saddle to the east, to face,
we used to say, the hospital
some blocks away where
he died.

II.

Next, the centerpiece, nobility raised high
above the rebel rabble, splendidly
in control, bareheaded, humble
in an aristocratic sort of way, not yet
dismounted bookish in the mountains,
still on the Saddlebred who would die
horribly of tetanus, but who would
outlive his rider, he of Grey Eagle stock
who bows eternally
to the south.

III.

Then, the statesman, politician, palm up and out
toward the great general back down

the avenue, leaning a bit off balance, not
quite trampling a book under his left boot,
embraced by an arc of Doric columns,
the traitors' exedra, over which soars
a fluted shaft topped by a draped woman
pointing to Heaven, a figure
that cannot be Victory, is
Liberty or Virtue. So we
used to say.

IV.

Farther along, we come to
Mister Unmovable, all hooves down,
four-square, unshakable, upright
in the saddle, he and his horse
fiercely glaring at the irritable traffic
to the north, glaring
forever.

V.

And then the clown-bald man
in the chair, not really a wheelchair,
who faces back east between the double
line of oaks, back to the generals, back
to his president, the one and only.
Above his head, the mapped globe
bobs on a boiling sea of shipwreck—
men and women, a dog, a bull,
a horse. Fish who are not there circle
the marble base, counter-relief,
as are the swallows. In his left hand
a scroll, in his right a pen. But he is not
writing, is not sketching, is staring

at nothing in our world, the hair
above his ears sweeping forward
like waves . . .

VI.

Finally, a pill of a pedestal, white
topped with brown bronze, a thin,
horseless man shows you his back, his
buttocks, holding above his flocculent
head a book, a tennis racket. Rising
from the ground below his feet, four
children, trapped at the waist, each reaching
with one hand for help, we used to say—
or to fend off a blow from the racket, from
the book. This man wearing our clothes
has turned his back on the commander,
on the generals and the politician, on
the rising sun. We used to stand to his left,
the south side of the street, so that the racket
formed a halo round his head. He sported
large spectacles, which he could lift
from those children to the western horizon,
direction of death, something we had
long before redefined as Manifest Destiny.

The South

Can't get out of my head
                that Ezra Pound was driven
down Monument Avenue by Harry Meacham,
        past Stonewall and Jeff Davis and lofty Lee,
past that plumed showoff JEB Stuart and on
                down Franklin to the Jefferson Hotel
to suffer the locals. That he chewed some genteel fat
        for over an hour, that James J. Kilpatrick
                said next day in print his talk was in-
        comprehensible, harmless, that this
odd duck should never have been locked up
                at all.

Not one of those bronze boys
                had been executed—
killed, sure, JEB and Stonewall, but not tried
                in a proper court of law, taken
        to place of execution and
                hanged pissing bug-eyed
or shot proudly through an unrepentant chest.
        What did he think
                as he passed them, the losers
        and the traitors nobled there in the sky,
                chins up in defiance, we said, forever?

Not even the literati
understood half he said that day. Pound had
                never lacked conviction,
        but often (so often), coherence. Thirteen
        years in the loony bin, more time
                behind bars than

43

Tokyo Rose . . . He'd danced and sung over
the Atlantic, above clouds
first time in his sixty years . . .
How many Richmonders does it take
to screw in a light bulb? I was asked
within a month of my arrival from Georgia.

Why don't West End women
take part in group sex? Good jokes,
even now, like all nasty cracks
with their smidgeon smear of truth.
Why the Parisians planted trees
along the Champs-Élysées . . . That's right,
so the Nazis could march in the shade.
How could he have done it
when he docked in Naples? Shading his eyes,
my ass. He gave the crowd
the Fascist salute, final sign this genius had learned

nothing, was still just, by gawd,
a brainy child of the First Amendment.
Beyond shame? Beyond Nietzsche?
The heart squeezed out by the mind, JR Lowell had said
of Edgar Poe, our hometown boy . . . Free
as the clouds are free. No record
Pound visited the Poe Shrine, though I've seen
a framed Gertrude Stein
in the Enchanted Garden. Or was that
Julius Caesar?

What hath a poet to do with politics? my Tertullian
keeps asking. Everything, nothing. In the Alps, in
the gondolas, did he think
of Richmond, its famous boulevard
a monument to the O So Lost Cause, the way I think

of Savannah spared by Sherman as a gift to Lincoln?
And Oglethorpe in his armor
and his swagger and his tricorn hat
puffing out his chest dead
center in a lovely square of live oaks and
chigger-infested moss named, if you can
believe it, after the enemy to the south . . .

EXHIBITION

Art never improves ...
—T. S. ELIOT

... if art is freedom of the spirit, how can it exist within
the oppressors?
—NADINE GORDIMER

[Paris] [New York] [Philly]

Brâncuşi's The Kiss *(1916)*

There's a war going on. Brâncuşi chips
at it yet again, number four, this more
simplified shape, this ultimate kiss for
John Quinn, this not-Rodin, no hip pressed
by a man's hand trailing toward bliss . . .
Lips locked, utterly equal, their eyes
nearly fuse. They need no noses, they
have breasts to press, heads flat and level
to host a pair of martinis. (*Do not touch.*)
And we do not. Still, we toast the smooth,
the rough, the limestone baselessness
of the artist's buss, this boot box essence.
What is it we make tonight? We patronize
the arts. We chat and share. We kiss the air.

Dalí Wins Wild Eyes Competition Against Ray

16 June 1934

They do it for Van Vechten, five years after the crash.
Of course, it's no contest. Ray looks focused, sure,
maybe a little angry. But Dalí has stepped out of Plato's Cave,
is the *Ding an sich,* Wildness Incarnate, something

    from a Dream—both men necktied, though Ray's
    in shirtsleeves (as they used to say), Dalí sporting
    a sport coat or suit coat with lapels huge to us,
    though the Spaniard himself's thin as a fantasy,

mustached, hair slicked back, coat hanging a bit off
Poe-ish sloped shoulders. Man Ray is all there, tangible,
more man than ray, could be a stock trader on the floor
in his white dress shirt, nose a little crooked, a boxer's,

    or American kid's with a history of wholesome
    schoolyard scraps. Dalí's shirt is garish for the day,
    even if the day dawns in Paris—aggressively striped
    behind the hatched tie. And he's taller, so much so

it's a shock to notice Ray's right shoulder's obscured by
Dalí's left—but, isn't bigger-headed Ray closer to the camera?
He leans pugnaciously forward, into our twenty-first century,
espresso and Rum St. James, let's say, on his breath.

    Erect Dalí's an Egyptian shape, abstracted into the
    extravagant, behind and not behind this Man Ray gent,
    a guy mugging with a celebrity friend he could never
    out-oddball. So what are *you* looking at? Have these boys

just now laid eyes on Adrienne Fidelin? Settle in. Open up.
It's Bloomsday in the city Joyce decamped to in order
to glare back at his hometown, to frolic in the great wide world,
to stay alive as long as he could.

How She Came to Be a Model

8 April 1973

The gray doctor ordered out of her clothes
while he watched her, had her walk the length
of the chilly room in the fluorescent glare.
She was nineteen. She thought all French doctors
did it this way. He touched her here, there, ungloved
fingers cold, she said, as the grave, gave her pills
he watched her swallow. He stood beside her
like a critic before a painting
he'd traveled a little too far to see.
On the crowded bus everyone was weeping,
the handsome woman's eyeliner running, tears
on the fungo of bread under an old man's arm,
light pooling in the tangled eyes of lovers.

Picasso, the old man said to her, *is died.*
Picasso, he said between tiny sobs, *is died.*
She was dizzy the rest of the day, dizzy
without wine in her little room with her
pretty sketches pushpinned to the walls, things
out of focus till nearly midnight. Then
he came to her, bald, of course, pot-bellied,
sun-damaged breasts leathery, hanging flat,
but still at first a man all angles, his pupils
huge and growing now, black as empty spaces
in x-rays, filling her room with the searing
blackness of being truly seen, blackening
her delicate, bland pictures—*Making me,*
she said, *finally nothing, nothing at all.*

Remedios Varo's *Locomotión Capilar* (1959)

Riding the bicycles of their beards,
        wearing wreaths of cloud, they come,
    they go, one roping the startled woman
      with his rufous anaconda whiskers.
Only she looks at you, her fingers
      splayed in surprise,
   lifted off the cobbles and balanced by
       the birds in the lower right

    who dive and swoop below the scholars'
(I say scholars) pointed shoes,
    in the ocher alley, the angled
confinement of the architecture, a triangle
      of dark sky trapped by walls
   and an arch. Starless, moonless.
    A maze, but the men
   are not amazed, their eyes serene,
contemplative, looking out of the frame, inward

   at nothing, while the fellow in the niche
      hoists the only woman, she whose eyes
   register fatigue and surprise, she
    who's being lifted
      out of the way so the scholars
can turn and turn again unhindered, un-
      distracted in the warm angles
of sterility, angles and arcs, and the birds, too,
live in the angles, even
    the birds live in the angles.

Bouguereau's Big Bow-Wow

Adolphe Bouguereau's Battle of the Centaurs and the Laphithae *(1853)*

My money's on the Centaur, yours
      on Mister Muscle with the perfect butt.
The Centaur's the force
           that splits the woman
     off from the man, the fierce face
that steals their faces, that pulls ours
          to the wall, handfuls
    of hooves freezing
the hero, turning the woman's eyes
         away from the human.

Caught between good intentions
    and really bad manners,
between angry sky and barren earth,
       I'd say the fit fellow's already Xed.
       The woman struggles
  feebly. But you say,

    The man's achieved the stasis
        of cultured concentration.
Yes, I say, *a perfect target for a club so cocked*
     that it will free
    this woman from her comely kinsmen—
long enough at least to stretch her
       horizons.

A pyramid for stability, you say.
      But the pyramid's apex
is the savage wedge that will destroy it.
   Balance, you say you see, *the beautiful man*
and the beautiful woman, joined

in a moment of—by an image of—
unity.

It's a battle scene, I say—*it's terrorism.*
            Dark struggles all around, bestiality
triumphant in the shadows. *It's lovely,*
        you say. And you say: *Hands sprout,*
thus tame, hooves. And, look: Is Mister Muscle
                growing up a tail?
        Faulty anatomy, I tell myself—but I hold
            my tongue, thinking,
        I can't help thinking,
                of yours.

Riefenstahl

... french horn, field
                 of fallen stonehenges—no—Greek
      debris, spooky ooze music, roofless
temple, more light now,
                overlapping rubble, wild
flowers, fallen columns, another shattered temple, another,
           rising reverent tones, sonorous masonry ...

      ... dissolve after dissolve, not one human figure here
Desolation
         Classical
              Central, more columns upright and the
camera's now moving now with
          purpose, pull-
      ing you through a doorway to the ult-
imate, the inner temple ... horn tri-

              umphant, epiphanic bright
          sunlight, so you're inside
the Parthenyawn: music (naturally) crests,
        shudders with pleasure, swings you
to the famous front: for a long, a LONG.
      STATIC. SHOT.

Nicked column flutes
      and geysering strings contrail
            above you, or-
chestral ecstasy eases, eases ...
        THERE: *A MAN'S HEAD!*
    (his empty eyes) more
           faces now, all
      marble, less

and less bat-
tered, brushed
by tender woodwinds, faces, fluent bodies
mist enfolded, invested, draped, touch them, smooth them,
as the camera turns
them

into

gesture . . .

Home Front

She hates
Savannah, hates her mother's
            unshakable strength, hates
that boy who sends her postcards:
KEEP US OUT OF WAR.
Lindberg, she heard a man say, a woman say,
                was a great man, was a traitor.
When the front page screamed WAR!
        even she was scared
            for a couple of days.
Japs killed 3,000 Americans.
                Where? And what were Americans
            doing over there?
                    Her mother
wheezed, boiling corn.
Broughton Street had a scarecrow wearing a button:
        KICK 'EM IN THE AXIS!
People're getting bad, her mother frowned,
        war's making them mean and low.
            She liked the big button
        on her father's torn coat
when he leaned into the room,
                a black badge with red letters:
TO HELL WITH HITLER.
She loved Daddy's crooked smile, but Mother
    made him leave again because he smelled
            like whiskey.
        She saw Santa on a poster
squeezing the air out of Adolph, stomping
                with one boot a bald Mussolini.
    Would she get anything
        she wanted this year?

Saturday Evening Post showed a boy her age
        holding a black comb to his upper lip,
    his other fingers shaped into a gun
at his own temple. None of her brothers thought
    it was funny. Hitler-boy
      had the happiest eyes!
        Nothing ever makes sense.
Nevertheless, seventeen, my father will leave the farm,
     will somehow survive Guadalcanal,
  somehow find this girl in Savannah
plugging wires into a board,
     and, eventually, somehow, they will
       make this poem.

Looking into Milano

Lowest birth rate in Europe, but Italians are, yes, skilled

in sensuality—foods, fabrics, frescoes, bronzes, marbles,
oils, foreplay. I'd left behind those icy clerks in Bern (never
saw a couple holding hands, never a single peck on a Swiss
cheek). On the Alpine downslope into Milano palm trees
rustled, caressed . . . Metro, then out into a vast piazza, my
first piazza ever: GLORY. Pigeons shit their welcome onto
my suitcase. Facing the duomo a long city block of ads
(aspirin to underwear to wine and watches)—but still, that
fantasy cathedral, smack on the site of the Roman basilica.

I drew sketches, took photos—when did I notice the couple

on the bench—that neither had leaned away even to gaze
into the other's eyes, had not separated lips in half an hour?
Gentle circling, barely bussing, as if conscientiously spreading
her lipstick . . . I circumnavigated the building that took seven
centuries to complete. Candoglia marble arranged Gothic-
ish, more like Disney than Renaissance. So was the couple,
still at it, lips lightly touching, lightly (not what you would
call kissing) when I cut through the Galleria to La Scala
where the fashionable loitered haughtily, a dozen or so
Carabinieri scanning the crowd, especially me, peering
down side streets in their killer Armani uniforms, strapped

operatically to black machine guns.
                                        I hiked across town.

Leonardo's famous failure, desperate eggshells of color
clinging to a mainly blank wall, Michelangelo's unfinished

Pietà, attenuated, hacked, nursing home futility slashed
all over it. Un panino al tonno, café doppio, and I limped
back into Piazza del Duomo to see *them,* my God, still at it!
Could it be the same couple? I checked my notes: same
shiny brown hair, black stilettos, leather coats, jade earrings,
his light gray wools with the stain at the crotch. I looked for
a camera crew, but this was no shoot, no stunt. Were they

robots? Never an auditory smooch. Ethereal, supernatural.

My testicles ached for them. I've seen cinematic kisses all
over Italy, but why this marathon right out in the open?
There was no tension or the slightest sign of strain. Was
it a *game?* More Brâncuşi than Rodin, they were level,
neither bent back like the helpless, swooning sailor's girl
in Times Square or like Canova's Psyche looped in Cupid's
reviving arms. Equality. Mutual tactile attention raised to
the level of prayer. *Devotion,* I whispered. Good Catholics,
let's say, they could wait for a wedding night. So, chapped

lips, blue balls, cramps, and spasms. Four hours? I wore

a stopwatch in those days, timed my walks, had seen
a Verona sidewalk festive with used condoms. I longed
to interview them. But they never opened their eyes.
Maybe they were blind? To this day I remember that
swirling not-quite-kiss better than the gold Madonnina
on the duomo's highest spire, better than the navigli
from the quarries of Lago Maggiore. As well as I remember
Ambrose's shocking corpse, a little skin, hair clinging
to his skull—noseless, dressed up in gold and jewels,
silks and satins, waiting for Judgment Day. Milano, yes,

I saw it all with my own lonely, secular eyes.

Poe in Rome

Let's say he gets there, somehow,
        after leaving, oh, Paris, with his head
  full of Byron and Piranesi, stretches
on the rubbled weeds of the Palatine,
       kneels an altered man, he thinks, hum-
bled amid Coliseum shadows, scratching *My very soul*
  thy grandeur, gloom, and glory in a small
        pad. He keeps his
           distance from St. Peter's
but haunts gold-garish Il Gesù hoping to meet a Jesuit
    who plays cards and speaks a little English.

He knows he shouldn't
        sample the local wine, but
the smell of garlic and sweat, crowds on the Corso
    so unlike healthy New Yorkers, Londoners—he
    finds himself
in the broken boat fountain, waking
to eyes that do not laugh, ugly mouths,
         stretched lips, black teeth—
    figs floating? No:
        neighborhood chamberpot . . .

Why can't he have a drink or two
         like everybody else?
   At San Giovanni, he steps away
      in horror from Galilei's
  top-heavy façade. What
if there's an earthquake? How many
    have been killed already by falling apostles?
He wanders tortured vicoli
    on the Field of Mars. He drinks

from a fountain of stone books. A street trapped
in Pompey's buried theater circles him back
                    to Satyr Square. *No,*
        no catacombs, he says to the youth reeking
                    with energy, wild with ebony hair.
I would see, though, he says,
                        the Temple of Jupiter
                the Biggest and Bestest and Caracalla's
        Baths, where Shelley scribbled Unbound.
Ah, the youth breathes, *but first I take you*

            to the No-Catholic Cemetery where you can,
                        ah, commune with the Anglo poets.
            Dupin's creator's moved, even trembles
                at the bitter water of Keats's words. Pyramid?
        Why a pyramid here? *Death pitches his*
                        whimsy-tent
in the city of eternal excrement, he mutters.
            The boy laughs too hard.
                        On the way back the cart climbs

            the Aventine, mangy horse
                    wheezing. Darkness seeps
        from every shrub, every
                        blackened stone.
    Piranesi's piazza: grandly funereal,
                symmetrical, pierced with obelisks,
    smacked with elaborate plaques, the whole
                    brooded over
        by cypresses. *Arancia,* the boy says,
                        slipping a warm slice of fruit

            into Poe's palm. His jaw hinges wince.
        He bends obediently to the keyhole. *San Pietro,*
            the boy says, *stupefacente.* But

Poe sees only a dark corridor
of hedges leading the eye to
a gray blank. *Nebbia,*
he would have said, if he had known
what he was looking at, if he had known
the word.

Drought, Rome

Thank God we're not there to see the fountains
dry. Hot enough in Trastevere even when
there's water everywhere. And when the men
hoist the Madonna through the streets, their sin
glistens on their grimaces, drops to the stones
named for St. Peter, flecks of sweat along
Via della Lungaretta that the throng,
crossing itself, ignores. It hurts my bones

to watch them, even the youngest straining
to keep the Virgin aloft. Before, they bend
to the *nasone* in the piazza; after,
kneel below the poet's marble spats
and iron cane. Pray today it's raining
and every silent mouth open to heaven.

Exhibition

This time through I see
> that (after the old lady
in the first room) I'm not
> > seen, the only eyes
> that meet mine dead
blanks of masks. And *now* I see
> > the anuses, so many, so
> lovingly, so puckishly
> > > placed, puckering.

> My cooing friends,
from so far away, see what I saw
> > the first time: huge hands
and feet, arms like water arcs, and still
> > none of us can find
the guitarist or the guitar. We all clap
> > > our flimsy palms
> > at the acrobat,
> > > > at the
> > > coalescing kisses.

Berth of Modern Poetry

E. P.

Can you believe Willyum the Wumpus
put up with me sixty years? Never
have another friend like him. Cautious, cagey.
Good listener. Got stuck in Amygism,
couldn't yank him out of her
huge tight ass. In fairness, he *tried* to bow-wow
the Big One. But that *Paterson,* big a mess
as my *Cantos*—well, smaller, but still
a mess.

　　　We were on the Penn fencing team
together, while all our tastes were keen,
you could say. Fencing made you think
with the other fella's head, feel
the other fella's muscles rippling
toward a specific action. We used épées,
heavy as they were, none of that flimsy
foil slinging. He was good. But I was better,
more aggressive, good at riposte. Boxing, stunned
ol' Champ once with a sharp counter-punch.
Bill—Bill was polite, even with a sword in his hand.

And now he's gone. "Struck of the blade /
that no man parrieth," I said once,
about some guy I made up. They won't let me
keep my fencing things here,
but I've still got 'em,
somewhere.

W. C. W.

Shit, I'm not gone. Sitting right here, wherever the hell
here is. Sure, I remember meeting Ez, the liveliest,
most intelligent, damndest *thing*
I'd ever come across. Talked poetry all night
in the dorm, nearly put my eye out
with his father's walking cane, thinking
that was fencing. I could have spitted him.
Should have. Sombitch thought he'd defeated
the whole fencing team he couldn't make, including
Leonardo Terrone, our coach from It'ly. Ez
was as bad a fencer as he was a dancer, cook, or carpenter.
Madox Ford said he played tennis "like an inebriated
kangaroo," though he was the only one of us
didn't really drink. Tennis didn't look like tennis
when Pound played it. He'd shout "Egad!" and wheeze,
sit down, jump up, jagged and surprising and slap-dash
as his homemade furniture. Ford did extra time jawing
in a Paris chair cause he couldn't get *out* of it!

Paris's where Ez traded lessons with Hemingway,
writing for boxing, boxing for writing, blow for blow.
Wyndham Lewis popped in and found them going at it
(Pound's fencing gear visible in a corner), said Hem
"without undue exertion" repelled one of the kangaroo's
"hectic assaults" after which "Pound fell back upon his settee."
1922, the year of litrachur's nuclear atrocities, Hem wrote
that Ez led "wit his chin" and had "the general grace
of a crayfish," whatever that means. That snake Hemingway
flattered and coddled our wild man till my friend
pulled *in our time* out of him and bullied a publisher
into launching Mister Macho—who then allowed as how
Ez had "developed a terrific wallop" in his private Paris gym.

From the beginning I let him be village explainer
to my village idiot. I had a lot to learn and he to teach
for all his affectations. Wrote to my mother that
Ez was the essence of optimism. Well, wadn't he?
Even in the loony bin he was the same guy
who taught me what poetry could be.
While failing history at Penn, he was *making* it,
even in drag in Greek drama, heaving massive breasts
in one ecstasy after another. Euripides,
that was. Genius? A genius passed through him—
a *presence*—from time to time . . .
He was a splendidly cracked pot, vase
beautifully cracked. Wit and profundity,
profundity and wit, with a huge serving
of plain bull shit.

Slow reader, never read the Rooshans, though
he still had opinions. Eliot said he knew
next to nothing about philosophy, theology,
even French poetry and fiction. How to describe
his intellect? "Desultory," he said more than once.
And intellect's only a slice, *edges* in the mind . . .
But who has a great mind anyhow? Not me.
"Prose for the detestable; lyric for the desirable,"
something like that, he said. Eliot? Too great
for his own good, probably. Bookworm.

All those pages . . . Maybe we left
too much space on each. Too often elliptical
too rarely erotic.

Did he go crazy? He was always
a bit of a nut, a pure product of America,
especially the First Amendment.

Ha! When Joyce asked his opinion about that
Work in Progress, he wrote, "Nothing short
of divine vision or a new cure for the clapp
could possibly be worth all the circumambient
peripherization." Though he helped JJ at first,
in the Bug House (and long before)
he was anti- the cult of Sunny Jim.

Whadya think of this:

> There, in the forest of marble,
> the stone trees—out of water—
> the arbours of stone—
> marble leaf, over leaf,
> silver, steel over steel,
> silver beaks rising and crossing,
> prow set against prow,
> stone, ply over ply,
> the gilt beams flare of an evening.

That's the left hook Hemingway could never teach him,
or learn. That's a Venice that can knock you out colder
than the real thing. His name means "help" in Hebrew
and he was that to all of us. Still: *energy.*
Ezra means *energy*
to me.

Orvieto

I.

Have you driven the switchbacks up the cliff?
Have you plunged into vicoli, eyeballed
your way toward the duomo? And if
you have, did you wedge the unscratched rental
for a night only, you thought, before the drop
at the airport and the train to Rome?
And did you love the town, and did you stop
every few paces for a photo of this dome,
that tower, the old lady taking her ease
in the shade, her chin on her polished cane?
Did Signorelli's *Antichrist* please
as much as the cobalt sky, lack of rain—
horrific pain in the night, EMTs, jostling,
swerving dark down the mountain—dying . . .

II.

"What a way to go," he whispered before they
slammed in, shouting for light, scolding them both
for the coldness of the room. On the way
down the mountain he made her take an oath
she would approve no treatment before
clearing it with his doc back in the states.

Hot. No A/C (no Wi-Fi), no one with more
than a smidgen of English. Had the Fates
snipped his thread, here, just down the mountain
from that heavenly hell, just a lover's leap

from Signorelli's masterpiece? What dumb
seed had he sown long ago, what crop to reap
here, punctured in paradise? His face began to burn.
Drugs dripped. What final lesson had he come here to learn?

Volterra

She was saying, "One arrives to the horrid
of the Balze . . . corrosion provoked by atmospheric
agents, steep and deep precipices . . . the Balze
terrible shelter for the desperation of so
many suicides . . . have engulfed . . ." But
there she was and there it was, falling away
below the walls toward the defenseless sea,
wasteland of sand and clay, crumbling even
as he watched, she, a daydream of his in profile
facing off against his nightmares . . .

"We go," she said, and walked—oh, she walked—
ahead: "Teatro Romano—*theater*—the curtain rolled up
in low, thanks to a complex system of telescopes . . .
dressed in marble, where the choir found its place,
therefore, . . . a double order of columns corinthian,
carrara stone, brought to light in the years fifty by
professore Enrico Riumi with opportune structural
interventions, in an epoch in which it was thought
that *work* therapy" (here she smirked) "might be
effective remedy for psychic throngs . . ."—and
she a dead ringer for that girl in Tallahassee
forty years before, down to that rousing, erect
posture and tiny wrinkles round her dry, ironic eyes . . .

. . . sweeping her lovely hand: "From the top of the
mighty blocks of tufa an unforgettable and unusual
show can be admired, as the result of the yielding of
the sandy, em, *layers* of the pliocene. Above all at sunset
the precipice engages unusual and suggestive colorations
when the shadows of the brooms, found on the gray
clays, gives the rosy blue off from the sky background.
There, beyond the abyss, on the frontal cliff tops, Badia
Camaldolese, assembled 1030 and surely abandoned
by the monks in the last century for fear that the building
will collapse . . ." Nothing made her smile like Volterra's
teetering on the edge of geological catastrophe.

❧

Regretting all the week's Negronis—". . . so, the building
of housing the Pinacoteca entertains the Pinacoteca and
the Civic Museum: Here are exposed important paintings
deriving from monasteries and city churches. Here, Room
Eleven—Ah! Displays the masterpiece of the Tuscan man-
nerism, the *admirable* "Deposition" of Giovanni Battista di
Jacopo, famous as the Rosso Fiorentino (em, 1494–1540),
genial and uneasy personality the Rosso performed this work,
definitely the highest expression of his talent, in 1521,
as shown by the inscription in low to the right on the
table here, see, on commission of the Compangia della
Croce di Giorno—Oh! *please,* no, no—*not* to touch." A
guard turned toward them—strikingly handsome, looked
directly into her gray eyes. And he was a sagging ghost again,
a phantasm who had gone to Italy to warehouse spolia.

The Assisi Poem, Finally

I. ROBBED IN ROME

Ponte! Ponte! he yelled—frantic,
bony, looked Tunisian, I thought, I
turned and found my small bag
gone.

      I'd been so careful, pulling up to
the front door of the Hotel Canada, literally
running the luggage into the safety of the foyer—
then, *Ponte! Ponte!* and that's it,
I was robbed.

        Delores said the other guy wheeled,
stooped, ran. I never saw *him.*

          "It's OK," I said,
"they'll find nothing but two memo pads
and toss them into a trash can. It'll be interesting,
I said, searching Rome's miniature dumpsters,
I'll get a poem out of it: *Roman Trash.*"

But Roman trash was just like American trash,
block after block, the usual discards, ordinary
containers, unvalued ejecta, mephitic waste.

The International Herald Tribune carried a story
about my minister friend—"Bob's in trouble again,"
Delores said, and there he was making Baptist waves
about the Jew who failed to get the job teaching
New Testament back in Virginia. "I will go

to the American Embassy," I said. "I will
file a police report."

            It hadn't hit me yet, still,
to this day, has not hit me: Six months of poems,
untyped, and the best travel journal I'd ever kept,
detailed, lyrical, gone into one of Rome's most
prosaic neighborhoods, gone, it is now clear, forever—
Gehen, gaan, gān, andato . . .

II. ASSISI

I had parked below the medieval wall, climbed
stone steps through arch after narrow arch, found
the cozy room hanging over the twisting scala.
In the forum: a temple of Minerva, right there:
you could touch it. One church on top of another
and a crypt below, the saint at home, the ceilings alive
with God and his angels, the earth a bubble of stone
filled with God's breath. And Francis's and Clare's.
Gazing at heaven makes your neck hurt. It was March
and it was cold. We reveled in porchetta close to a fire,
overlooking the church ghostly at night. On the way home—
home!—Delores heard music and voices behind
a dirty blanket we pushed aside to find
Geoffrey Rush shining on the faces
of a small audience. We'd never heard of him.
He was speaking Italian, except
for his lips.

            One day we climbed on up
the mountain, had a picnic at the Rocca Maggiore.
What we ate I can't tell you or when that week
we made our tiny room a chapel. Maybe the Tunisian
learned English by studying my notebooks. Friends

joke I should search for poems set in Richmond
and Assisi, published under the name Ahmed.
Minerva, Francesco, Clare, Pomodoro, Vino della Casa,
I worshipped as much as the next guy in this place
of splendid food and tourist trinkets, this place
where gewgaws have been holy for 700 years.
I remember the hot fire to my right, crackling, the
church to my left in the pale moonlight, the bed
hanging over a scary Piranesi staircase, Francis's
sarcophagus glimpsed through a grille—*ferro battuto*—
garlicky smoke, onion armpit hiss of rain on marble . . .

Memory's a liar, we all know it. My notebooks
could have given you the textures and flavors, spices,
liqueurs, foot pain and shivers, shadows and whispers,
slick paving stones, gusty grievings in the Stevensy rain,
lichens, sacred caresses, hip bones, so much tasted
with reverence, touched
with love.

III. POLICE REPORT

Six months after we'd been there, the ceiling fell
in the earthquake, Doctors of the Church crushed
two Franciscans and a couple of restorers.
It was on television, Giottos in a storm
of stone and dust. In Richmond we literally wailed
and sobbed. So much lost, so much
gone forever.

　　　　　At Termini station I filled out forms.
The female Carabinieri there in those
killer uniforms had little English but soulful,
understanding eyes. The first one
called out a second one and I told it all again

in my mixed English and Italian,
both of them with sorrowful expressions,
shaking their lovely heads and
cooing, mournfully. Then two more came out
to hear of the American poet
whose poems had been stolen, to see him. And
a travel diary about Assisi.
Oh! Assisi! Auanto sia doloroso! Troppo male,
così male! Mi dispiace tanto!
Una tale sventura! Sei mesi di poesie!
they might have said. I remember
only their operatic sympathy, their
shapes in those uniforms, dark eyes.
I was young and didn't know it.
I'm old now.

      He had bright, ecstatic eyes,
onyx, crazy. He was very skinny, the bones
of his face all right there—St. Francis would have
pitied him, no doubt. The current pope would have
washed his feet, would have kissed them, the first
Jesuit and the first pontiff Francis—our bridge
to what?

      Six months of poems
and Assisi sung, Assisi set down
    in detail. Why
haven't I hated him? Why
      hasn't it pierced me?
   Not yet, not yet.

Salamanca

Eat days? Oh, *heat wave* she just said
in my own language. I'd say a dryish wavelet
in sultry Savannah or even in Richmond, but
miserable enough walking, for sure. Local beer's

cold, if uninspired. Seems nobody here knows
how to make a Manhattan or a Negroni, not
that you'd want one till the sun goes down.
All over town white storks clack on chimneys,

bristling nests bewitching bell towers.
Disguised Frenchmen from Paris, she says
then laughs at her own wit. I jot a note to look
this up. The new cathedral's astronaut floats

in the sandstone void near today's morning-
shift beggar, a bulky butterfly out of his
blackened palm . . . Above our glistening brows,
all around our revolving heads, Salamanca

glows gold beneath flawless cobalt. Lord,
grant each *charra* under heaven only the babies
she wants, and let us simmer in Salamanca
a few days more. Let drenched me slog

the steep *calles* rather than lean and loaf
in screenporched Georgia or hammocky Richmond.
I have descended to the Puente Romano,
guarded by its faceless boar, and climbed back

in summer slow motion to Plaza de Anaya where I
caught what was left of my breath. When Hannibal
mounted that hill in 220 BC, I choose to believe he
wheezed, at least a little. Iberians, Celts, Romans,

Visigoths, Moors, Frenchmen, Fascists—think
of all the blood beneath these stones.
Columbus slept here, scheming, his dreams
full of bad maps. . . . Delores booked a room

with a balcony on Plaza Mayor, big room blissful
with A/C and a firm, obliging bed—and, after dark,
visions of order and elegance that sink deeply
into savage senselessness. Past the cafes, bars,

restaurants thrumming with their medleys of tapas,
clutches of smoking students in their unlined,
intelligent faces, past bright museum banners, under
cigüeña blanca soaring, gliding, having given up

the arduous voyage to Africa, searching now for
urban scraps, this old heart flails erratically away
on its vintage drum set, its measure a scatter of
iambs, anapests, dactyls, trochees, quail exploding

from cover, Bobby Hendricks getting off two shots
whatwhat before I can raise my barrel. I am
fifteen years old and have never heard of Salamanca.

Don't Know Much About the French I Took

I silently disapproved when they said, "Let's go French
Miss Buckshaw," though I do know that I love you
for trying, even with your embarrassing Deep
South pronunciation, to get me to parle français.

I apologize now for my inability to talk turkey here,
for being so in the dark in the City of Light
and for imagining your sour breath and slipping
dentures, your ancient, phlegmy spit. I remember
"Fermez la bouche," not, I think, ever directed
at mute me. And "Ouvrez vos livres" comes back
in a Georgia accent, we all said so, even
the tongue-tied. Danny and Becky and Marsha,
the popular kids, made A's, I think now, and were
merciless in the halls before and after your class
where I sat in a fog of daydreams and discomfort.
I wonder how many times they've been to Paris,
if they were ever able to talk Sartre on the rue
du Whatever, if they are, still, even now,
high-school cool. Miss Rickshaw, Miss Buckshot,
you never showed me even a small kindness, but
I suspect you'll forgive me now for a mouth
full of English and the occasional, inappropriate burst
of desperate Italian. So: Merci, Madame, Merci.

And forgive me, Mrs. Dunham, for saying in class
that my little sister could write this Hemingway crap,
for thinking that "Big Two-Hearted River" was about
camping and could use some Byronic boffing
and Faulknerian flair.

                              Of course,
I didn't really say those things out loud,
but I did imply them, preferring showmen
to shell-shocked fishermen. Shelley's "The Cloud"
and Byron's "Prisoner of Chillon" were my touchstones
in those days. Forgive me for raining on
your professional parade. You were kind to me,
a chronically late, horrifically self-conscious
teenager, said I might be a writer one day. Grazie mille,
and ti prego, perdonami, Mrs. Dunham, Miss Buckshaw.
Rest in peace, wherever you are. I turned out all right,
I guess, in the end—if this is the end.

THAT BEAUTY

There is the falsely mystical view of art that assumes a kind of
supernatural inspiration, a possession by universal forces unrelated
to questions of power and privilege or the artist's relation to
bread and blood....

—ADRIENNE RICH

Birds, bees and flowers . . . have boundaries. . . . They are *objets
trouvés*, jewels, treasures, whose perfection seems to radiate from
themselves, as from an inner light.

—ROGER SCRUTON

October's Mortal Joy

We've got goldfinches this year,
who hang on the feeder upside down, and today
the sky's been full of sailing ships and icebergs
floating in the deepest blue. No wonder the air
has an edge and the greenest leaves are looking
a little let's say silver. Chipmunks—five of them!—
were hard at play after our breakfast, right here
on the still rich grass. Where'd this new baseball
on the patio come from? This gust of sadness?

Cricket, finch, squirrel, neighbor's dog
chirps, sings, stutters, barks. Those silver linings
in the southwest could blind you, there in the tree gap
where the sun wears a tattered bank of dark cloud
like Zeus robing himself in mortality for yet another
divine seduction. The dogwood in the corner's

all over red, shivering with anticipation
of throwing down her clothes of flame to become
Semele's blackened bones.

Her Garden

She tettered in a bigness
the tight buds made, breathless to
squeeze herself down
through trembling fingers,
narrowing, like her eyes, toward the
proper caring size she despaired of
ever reaching. I'm too clumsy, she said,

weaving spells of touching invisible
to me as the atoms in the flour
in the borrowed cup I held. She groomed each
reluctant leaf with bows and whispers,
leaving the plot
on a Sunday for one brief visit to a flame,

returning in a pale, sisterly hand
in an urn from her own mantle.
Spider web wishes in faded ink
have brought her back in all
her gray persistence to float
on the twilight air
behind her brightened house,
dusting the healthy yellow roses.

Lucky Strike

Verticals descending, left to right, that
brick smokestack (brown cigarette), then,
dead center, a rocket of a tank, (rusted
watertower), next, the smaller tank, shrunk
by perspective, pale blue, cleaner (newer?)
and closer to the bland blocks of a city
dwarfed by this has-been industry
in the middle distance, factory dwindling
from, at the stack's base, towers' skinny legs,
the foreground's lushness: notional trees, trees
like a roiled ocean or virescent clouds or pillows
or party balloons fallen from that unpolluted
sky, sky brushed lightly by wisps of cirrus . . .

Local Color

The poet who ran the red light
claimed he couldn't take his eyes off
that incandescent hickory
in the median across from
the Baptist preacher's house.
The preacher said, "I was doing

military press in my sunroom,
so I saw the whole thing. That
beer truck
had the green and that purple hearse
just slammed right into it. They was
books and beer everwhere. The whole
neighborhood smelt awful.
What hickory?"

All-Boys School, or This Limeless Gin & Tonic, My Prison Fare

with no apologies to Samuel Taylor Coleridge

Missed the student-faculty softball game,
another rout where two actual women
caught well-hit shots to help the old guys
astonish and infuriate yet again the young.
Every spring it's the same.

                        Overconfident,
misogynistic, increasingly disgusted, quarrelsome,
the nearly done seniors squirmed in a series
of smooth snares laid by the slow, the fat, the gray,
the canny, who went about their business,
cheerfully, respectfully.

                        So I'm told. This year
before the warmup, I limped home
and drank right here under the dappled dogwood
on the patio. Frayed cartilage and a thorn
of dead bone whine in my left knee.
Not to mention.

                        Three chipmunks streak singlefile,
slotcars, right under my chair. A cardinal flares
on the feeder. A mourning dove flutes
her five sweet notes.

                        And right this minute I'm missing
Ultimate Frisbee, where the young, muscled members
of my department prefer to be skins, but distribute
themselves fairly in a game they claim's more

about process than product. I toast their cries sifting
through the sassafras and cypress.

                                           It's OK.
I like it here where the goldfinch dazzles.
I've got a gazing ball tipped up by calla lilies.
And a fifth of Hendrick's in the freezer.

H.D.

E. P. IN THE GARDEN

Up the big maple
into my brother's crow's nest,
      the house hidden by leafy branches . . .

Beyond the hedge occasional cart, carriage,
      every half hour, a rattling tram
jolting past . . . He must not miss
      the last car, the train to Wyncote.
      "There's another
in half an hour." "Ah, Dryad," he says . . .
      We sway
      with the wind, with the clouds . . .

Finally, finally, we slide, slip through the branches, leap
      together to the ground, the solid ground.
"No," I say, "no," drawing back, a girl
      of my time and place.
      "I'll run ahead and stop
the trolley, quick, get your books, whatever
      you left in the hall." "I'll get them next time,"
he says. "Run," I say, "run." He just
      catches it, nearly falling, the trolley, swaying . . .

Now, I face them in the house,
      Father winding the clock, Mother
saying, "Where were you?
      Didn't you hear me calling?
Where is Ezra Pound?"
      "Gone." "Books? Hat?" "He'll get them next time."

HILDA WAS TOO TALL FOR A WASHABLE FROCK

Her mother wished dresses could fit her
"the way they did other girls." Toweringly embarrassed
        in Wanamaker's, Bonwit Teller's, she was
savage on the basketball court.

    Nothing fit her but Ezra, turret of classics,
    torrent of words, who would climb
        the lofty maple in her parents' garden.
Another's beating heart, another's breath, clang
        of the trolley beyond the hedges. They
stretched out in the crow's nest her brother had built.

    How he ached to kiss her, how she ached.
        He frightened her every time he caught the last
possible trolley, wildly swaying, nearly falling, waving, shouting,
        "I'll pick up my hat, the books next time!"

Last Autumn

Slow as we were, near the hill's top we had to pause,
　　　　　　seek the breeze in a clearing.
　　　Maples and woodbine,
oaks and hickories and dogwoods all flamed
　　　　　or glowed in the heavy air.
　　Dad fought for breath, beginning
　　　　　to look scared, but Mom still smiled
　　　her new half smile at the trees
　　　　　as if their fireworks
celebrated her recovery, such as it was.

That's when the birds came,
　　　　　a cloud of smoke-
colored waxwings, passing low over us, songless,
　　　feathers soughing, sighing so close
　　　　　you could feel
their going like a lover's breath on your face,
　　　like a mother's Sleep tight.
　　　　　　　Dad was busy wheezing,
　　hands on his knees, so he didn't say
　　　his predictable Don't look!

　　Mom, still as a tombstone,
was looking, head cocked to the shushing
　　　　　as if taking in a final message
　　about the virtues of silence.
The sky came back and on we climbed.
How can an addled, crooked smile be girlish?
　　　Then she bent double, hands on her knees:
　　　laughing at the puce drool
on Dad's shoulder, the high, splintered

laugh she'd always had. Odd, the things you don't need
words for. She laughed
at the only man she'd had luck
and courage enough to love, old Marine
who took the hill now with the heart
that saved the world
from burning down before I was born, and there I was
laughing with her
and pointing, as if a man's dignity

were nothing but colorful shit from the sky,
the chevrons and medals
of mockery—till he turned,
red-faced and hooting himself,
and we were all three whooping
and crying, like heroes trying to sing
in the executioner's flames.

Away

—A. E. HOUSMAN

We were talking the usual bull, beers
in hand, the air light, the light like air,
the river full of light, full of fish,
Don said, and I had said something
about teaching and Jack chuckled, "Yeah,
that's what Emerson said, first job
of the teacher's to inspire." That was
Aw Shucks Jack, with his mountain
accent deeper than that river, warmer
than the East Tennessee breeze.

He hadn't played half-rubber with us
that day, the pastime I hauled up from
Savannah to inflict in an apple orchard
on those middle-aged boys from Wisconsin
and Pennsylvania and by God Maine, but I
reminded Jack of the softball game from
a decade before when he had rounded third
like a runaway freight, belly ballooning
from the turn, and scared the catcher away
from the plate he hit with a slide that took
all our breaths away.

           Broom handle (wood),
solid rubber ball (baseball size, cut down
the middle), items just about impossible to find
in 21st-century Johnson City. And now I think
Jack did play, had the surest hands of the lot,
a born half-rubber catcher right there
where the river moves almost silently past

95

the orchard and all around the mountains lean in,
lean in as the light seeps away and darkling Jack
claps his palms together, grins, holds up
between thumb and forefinger half a ball,
and the old boy from Maine's still untwisting
himself to see if he really is out.

That Beauty in the Trees

You have a life brimming,
              you like to say,
         with truth, beauty, goodness,
and health, a life of not exactly poverty, and you
       are not really old. This November day,
        you and your love turn early
from the keyboards and ringing phones and go
              walking hand in hand
        through the respectable neighborhood.

Have the leaves ever been brighter?

        Someone
      is burning the fallen ones
against the law, or is that your
      happy childhood
    curling out of the deepest layers of your brain?
(You do not think "soul.") Maybe you say,
    "That beauty in the trees was always there.
It's just that the fullness of living had
      hidden it." Your love smiles as if to say,
    Tell me more, O professore!
Therefore, you do: "I mean, the various greens
          were their active lives, their
      consuming of the sunlight,
           their making of the molecules
    that keep them going."

And now, the florid maples

          sprayed with amethyst,
     ocher oaks and crimson dogwoods,

incandescent jasmine of the hickories,
carmine fan
of this sassafras flaring
in the Salmacis-clutch
of a scarlet woodbine can
thrill any lovers' stroll into baffled tears.

Why can't we feel this all the time, whatever it is?

After a while, you might say, jauntily,
to recover the lightness, "The trees
have lost their relentless greenbacks, begin
to live on their small pensions,
prepare to become winter's
dark skeletons, and so
the yellows and vermilions and magentas, the
flashing dazzles that have been there all along
flame out like—what?—like the spirits
of honest old men
who wear their wives' useless breasts, like
the spirits
of strong, tender women who've grown
wispy mustaches."

She likes the men and women becoming each other.

Spirits, she says,
with the sidelong look that means
now you must say,
"Sure. In their eyes sometimes, but
your whole life
is a kind of retina: You can see their spirits,
even if spirits can't survive
the death of the flesh. Anymore than these colors
can survive December."

For the moment,
you believe what you're saying.
And are there such good people? "Oh, yes,"
you have to say,
"for all your smiling. The ones
not like us: the quiet, simple people who've
struggled every day
for their food and clothing and shelter,
who've lived only
for their children
and grandchildren."

And who turn now away from the sunlight,

you suddenly want to say,
because it turns away from them,
and who begin
to burn with
the deep, silent anger
that we must say, we do say, we will always
say is a kind
of beauty.

NOTES & DEDICATIONS

"Troilos": Dedicated to Peter Schertz.

"Franz Kline's *Zinc Yellow* (1959)": Dedicated to Mary Jean Kledzik.

"*Estadio Guillermón Moncada*": Dedicated to Bill Hamby.

"The Ancrene Wisse": *The Ancrene Wisse* is a "Guide for Anchoresses." This more or less found poem is extracted from Mary Wellesley's "This place is a pryson," a review of the book *Hermits & Anchorites in England, 1200–1550*, ed. by E.A. Jones. I found Wellesley's review in *The London Review of Books*, 23 May 2019, pp. 3–6.

"Lily, Her Men": In memory of my grandmother, Lily Purvis.

"Founder": Thanks to Ted Kooser and William Logan for helping me evaluate and reconsider this sequence's tones and procedures.

"Suitor": Dedicated to Cliff Dickinson.

"Master": This found poem is taken from a letter by George Washington that can be located in Henry Wiencek's *An Imperfect God: George Washington, His Slaves, and the Creation of America*, 2003; in Sebastian De Grazia's *A Country with No Name: Tales from the Constitution*, 1999; as well as online at https://founders.archives.gov/documents/Washington/02-07-02-0300 and elsewhere. "Master" is dedicated to Rhett Forman.

"Public Servant, Country Squire": This material and direct quotation were taken from The Mount Vernon website on 16 July 2019 at "https://www.mount vernon.org/george-washington/facts/washingtons-teeth/george-washington

-and-slave-teeth/. Except for the information from Wiencek (*An Imperfect God: George Washington, His Slaves, & the Creation of America*, 2003), much of this poem is from "Did George Washington's false teeth come from his slaves?: A look at the evidence, the responses to that evidence, and the limitations of history" by Kathryn Gehred, 19 October 2016 http://gwpapers.virginia.edu /george-washingtons-false-teeth-come-slaves-look-evidence-responses-evi dence-limitations-history/. The speaker in this piece finds himself struggling with both horrific historical fact and transparent "scholarly" rationalization.

"How It Was": The futuristic speaker remembers Monument Avenue in Richmond, Virginia, before all its monuments were removed long, long before the utterance of the poem. The monuments were (in order, from east to west) JEB Stuart, Robert E. Lee, Jefferson Davis, Stonewall Jackson, Matthew Fontaine Maury, and Arthur Ashe. The speaker recalls what the statues looked like but not the names of people they represented. Or maybe he just doesn't want to say. The epigraph from *Hebrews* is (at this writing) still engraved on the western side of the Arthur Ashe Monument. "How It Was" is dedicated to Brent Baldwin.

"Dalí Wins Wild Eyes Competition Against Ray": Dedicated to Michael Taylor and Madeleine Dugan.

"How She Came to Be a Model": Dedicated to Sue Hayn.

"Remedios Varo's *Locomotión Capilar* (1959)": Dedicated to grandson Russell Byrd Smith and granddaughter Molly Thompson Smith, artists and jokesters.

"Riefenstahl . . .": See the opening few moments of Leni Riefenstahl's film *Olympia* (1938). This piece is in memory of Irby Brown, who knew his Riefenstahl as well as he knew his Ibsen and Strindberg.

"Home Front": In memory of my mother, Mamie Lee Purvis Smith.

"Poe in Rome": This piece mixes into the cityscape not only some Poe/Byron/ Keats but a bit of anachronistic Yeats. "Poe in Rome" is dedicated to Giuseppe Albano.

"Drought, Rome": Dedicated to Sari Gilbert.

"Exhibition": The Virginia Museum of Fine Arts' 2011 exhibition *Picasso: Masterpieces from the Musée Picasso*.

"Berth of Modern Poetry": Dedicated to Mary de Rachewiltz, this piece finds William Carlos Williams and Ezra Pound at rest—more or less—in a vague sort of afterlife. The nine-line quotation near the end (page 70) is from Pound's Canto XVII.

"Orvieto": An early draft of "Orvieto" (as two separate sonnets) was commissioned for a one-time oral presentation (with musical accompaniment) by Amherst Glebe Arts Response. On 22 October 2017, the sonnets were read aloud by Lynn Hanson as part of a concert in Amherst, Virginia. "Orvieto" is dedicated to Lynn Kable and Rick Gergoudis—the former for pushing me for sonnets, the latter for helping to keep me alive in Italy.

"Salamanca": Dedicated to Dave Cappella and Peter Liebregts.

"Don't Know Much About the French I Took": The title of the poem and part of line 2 are from "Wonderful World," recorded by Sam Cooke.

"Lucky Strike": This poem responds to a painting (oil on canvas) by Emma Knight. It is dedicated to the artist.

"All-Boys School . . .": Dedicated to Don Johnson.

"E. P. in the Garden": Drawn primarily from H.D.'s book *End to Torment*.

"Hilda Was Too Tall for a Washable Frock": Drawn primarily from Barbara Guests's *Herself Defined: H.D. and Her World*, as well as H.D.'s *End to Torment*.

"Last Autumn": In memory of my father, James K. Smith.

"Away": In memory of Jack Higgs.

"That Beauty in the Trees": Dedicated to Delores.

CPSIA information can be obtained
at www.ICGtesting.com
Printed in the USA
LVHW031206060423
743650LV00003B/483

9 780807 177983